BE
KIND.
by ellen

rover

RoverWorks.org

Every year, millions of cats and dogs enter animal rescues in the United States. Approximately four million pets are euthanised every year. That's one death every eight seconds.

Most of the pets featured in *Rover* once lived in a rescue and some were homeless when they were photographed for the book. *Rover* illustrates that healthy, smart, playful, unique, loving and confident purebreds and mixed breeds are available for adoption from rescues everywhere.

We hope these beautiful cats and dogs inspire you to welcome a rescue pet into your home.

Our mission is to reduce the homeless animal population by raising funds and bringing awareness to effective rescues with comprehensive spay and neuter programs. *Rover* has generated donations of over $2.5 million to animal rescues across America. Visit RoverWorks.org to learn more about our efforts and how you can see your dog in a future edition of *Rover*.

Rover is dedicated to all pets and those who love them.

Autumn

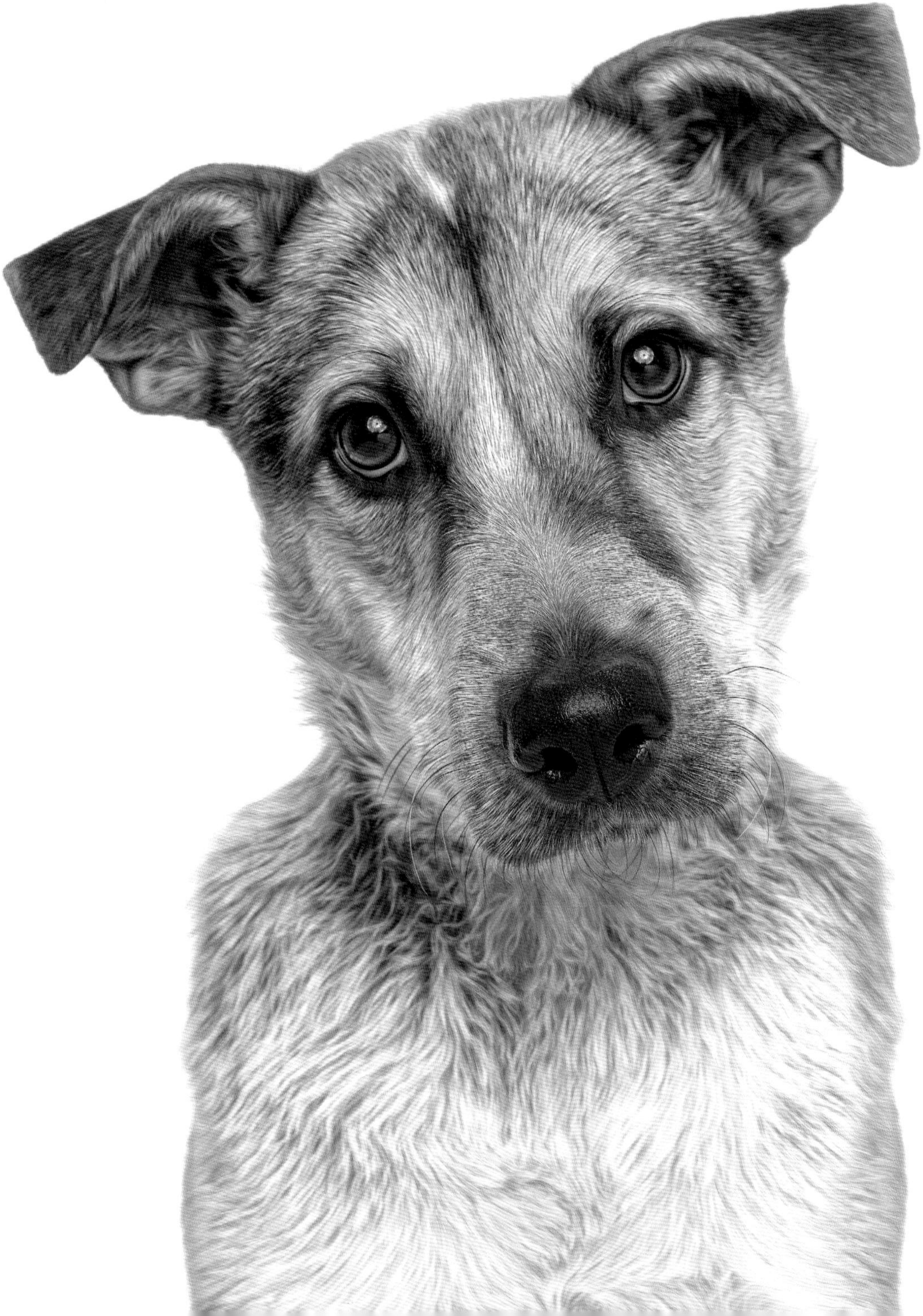

Wickett & Ashar

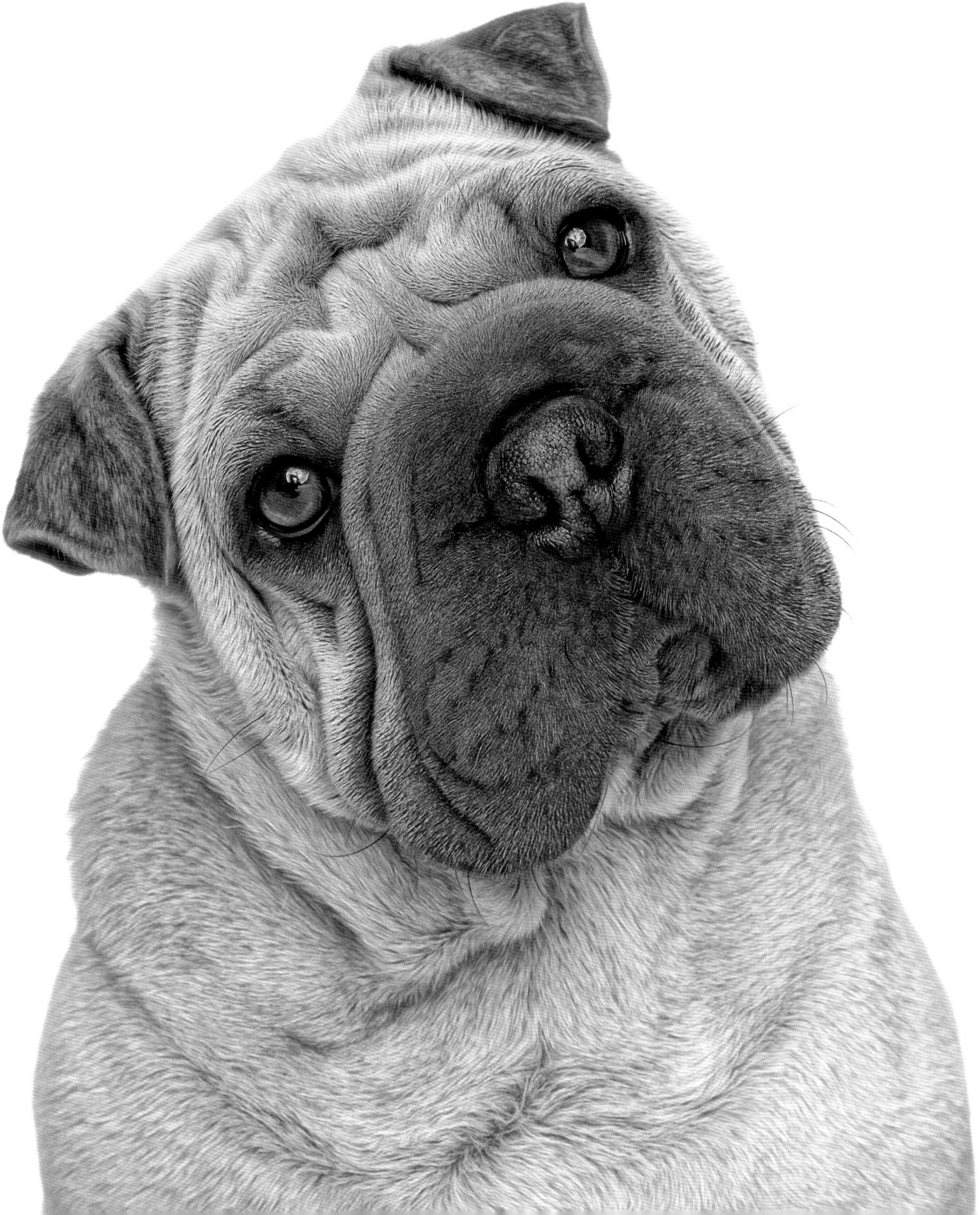

Sponsored Homeless & Lucy

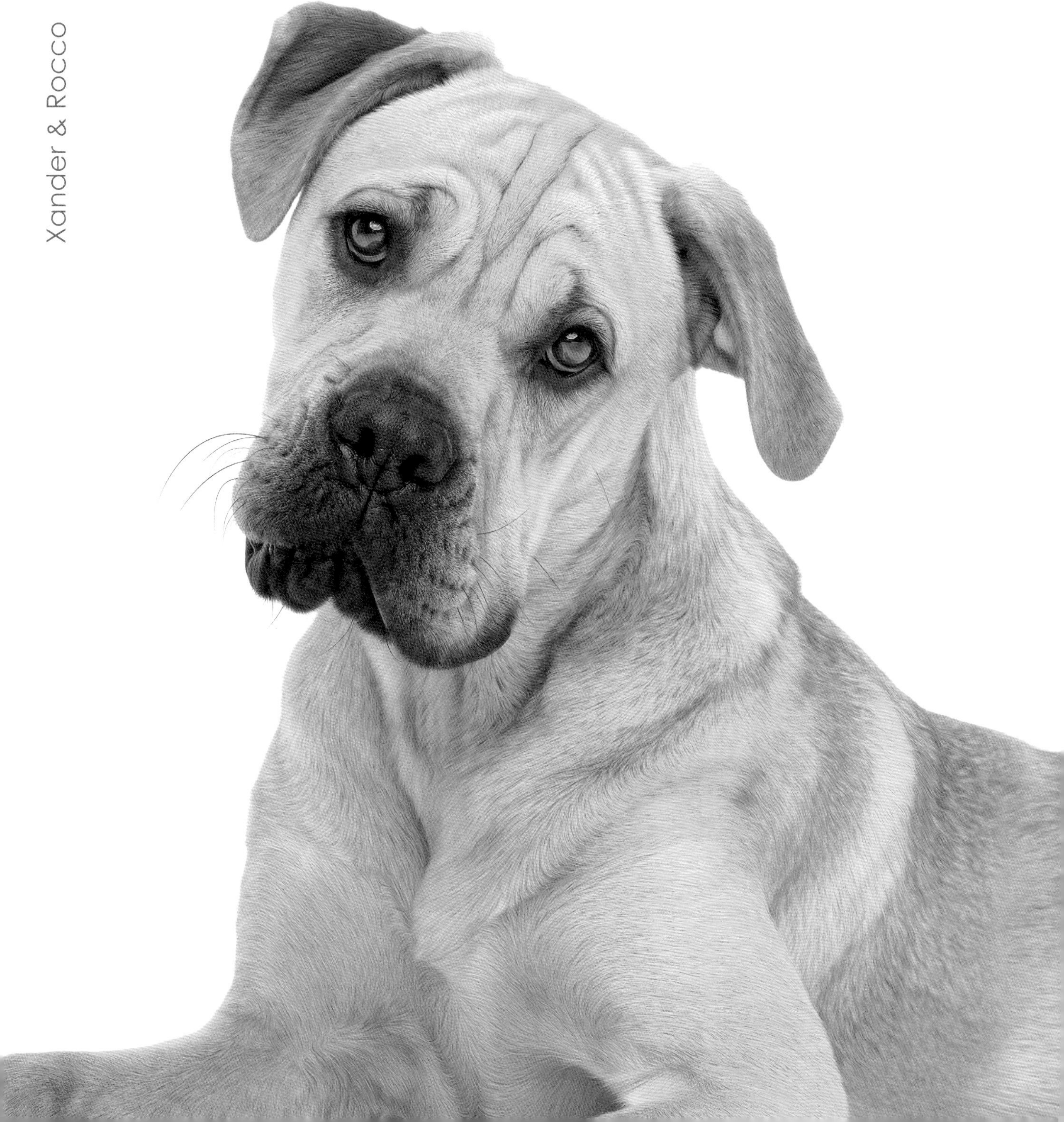

Xander & Rocco

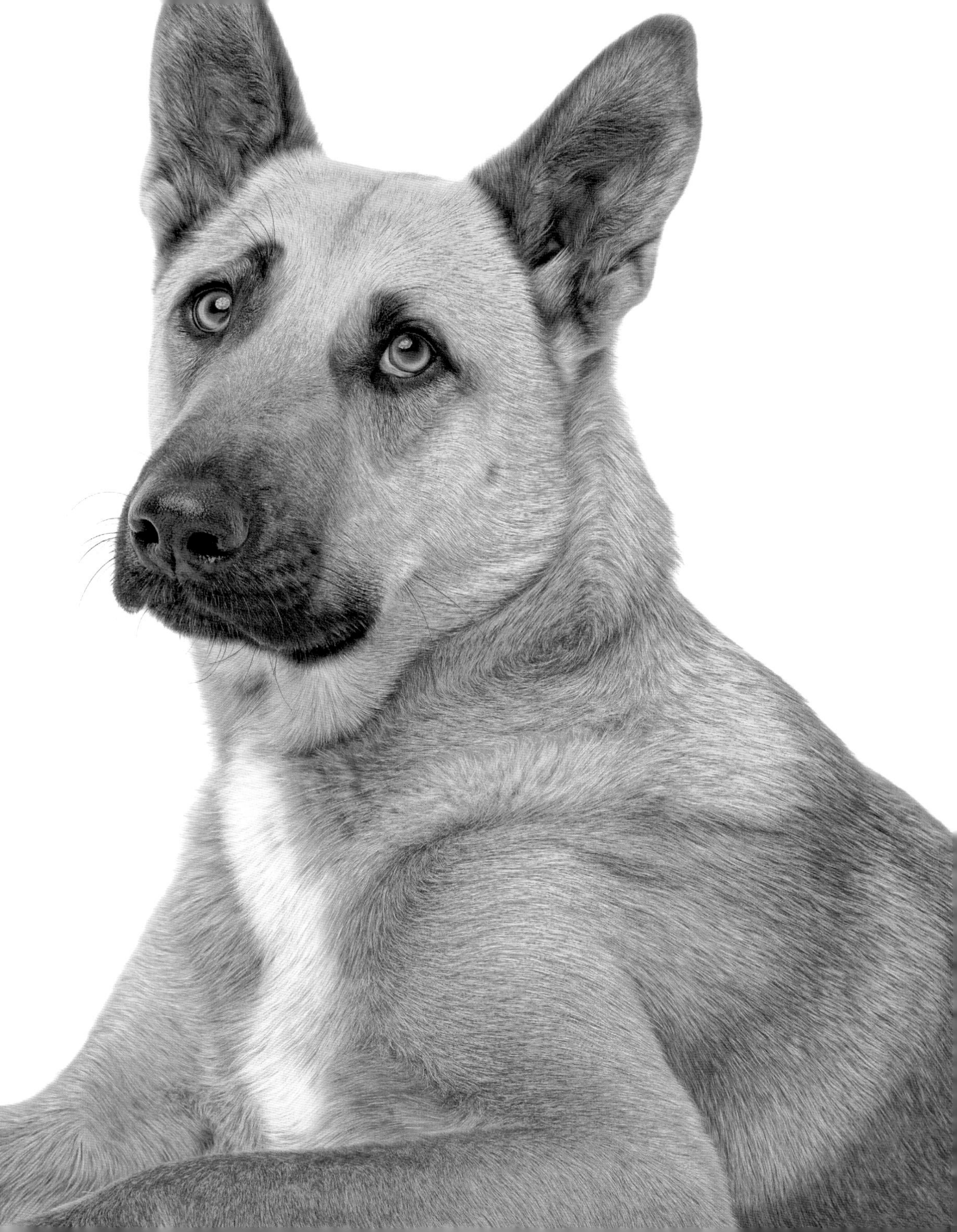

Willa & Milo

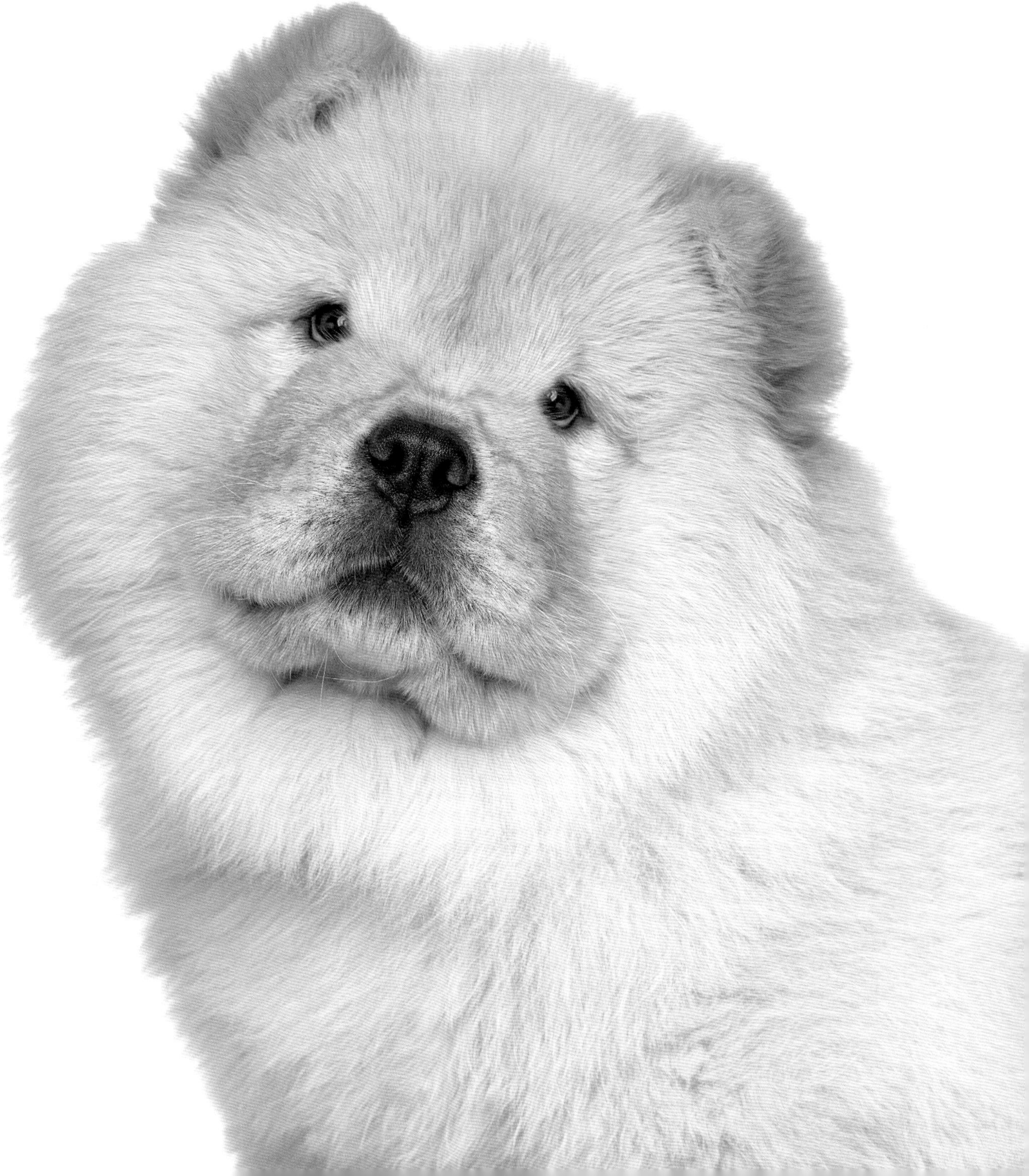

Theo & Chia

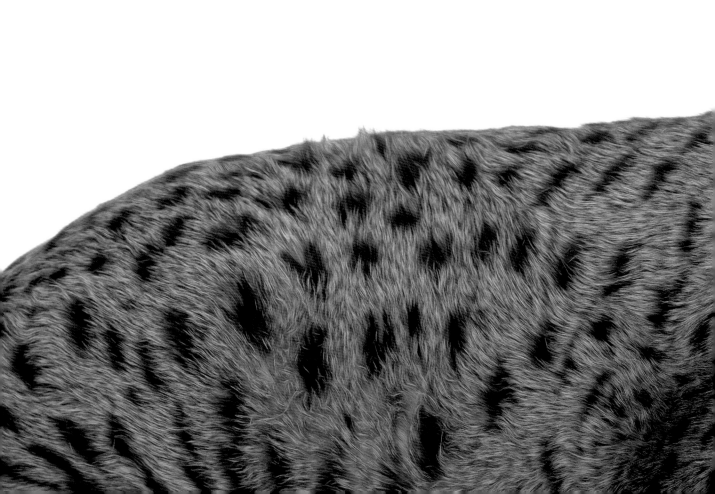

Freddy & Max

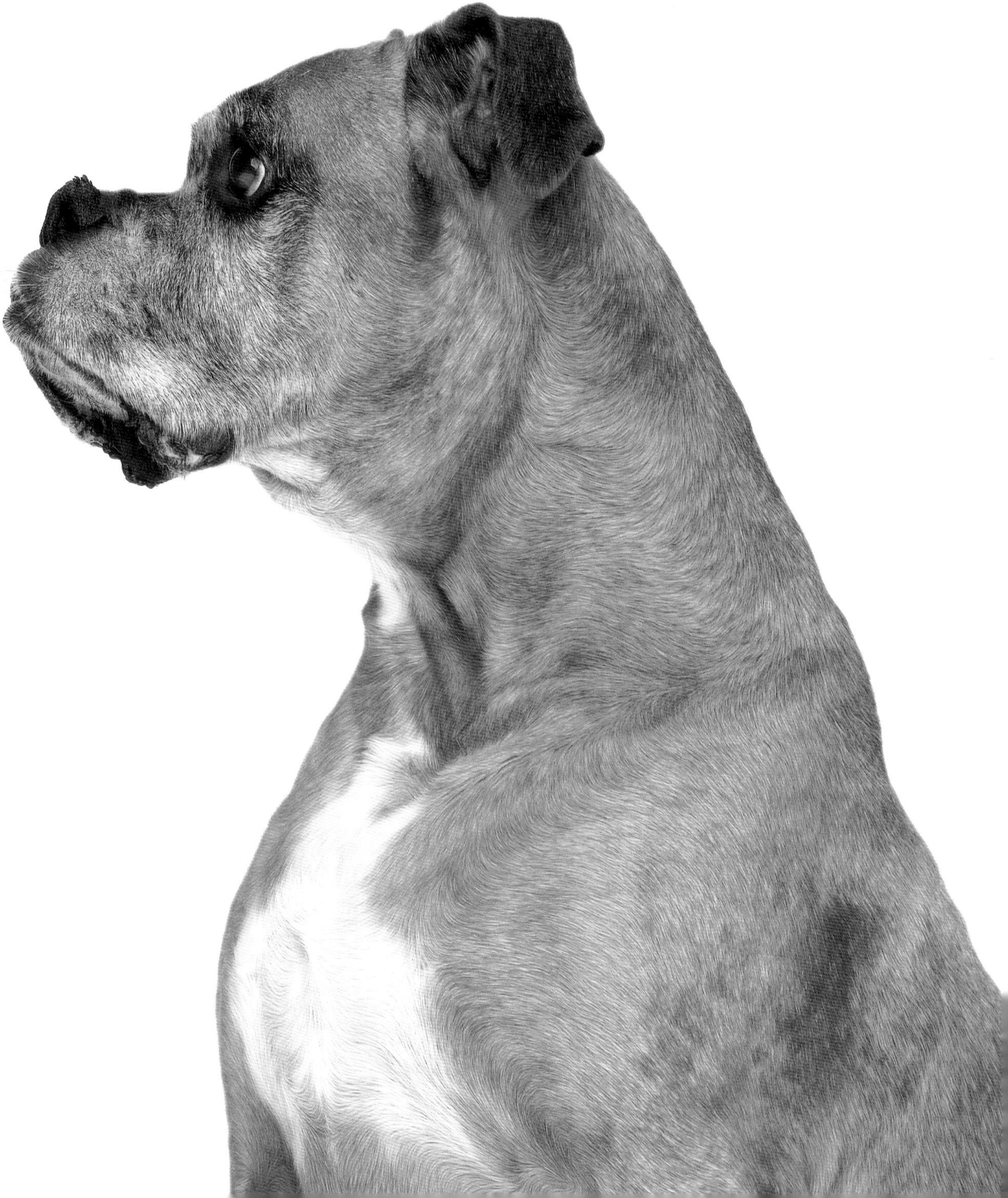

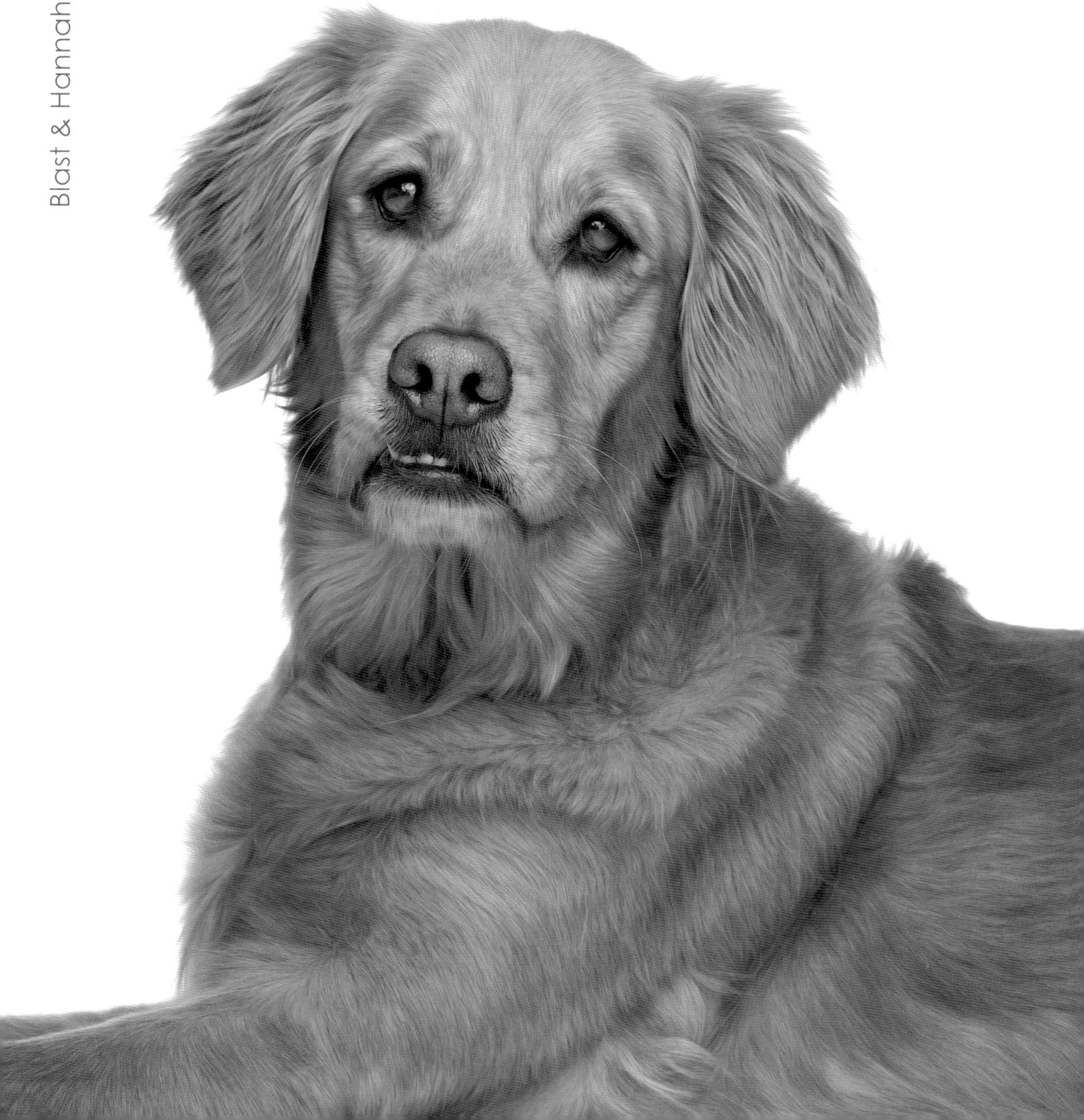

Blast & Hannah

Miko & Sammie

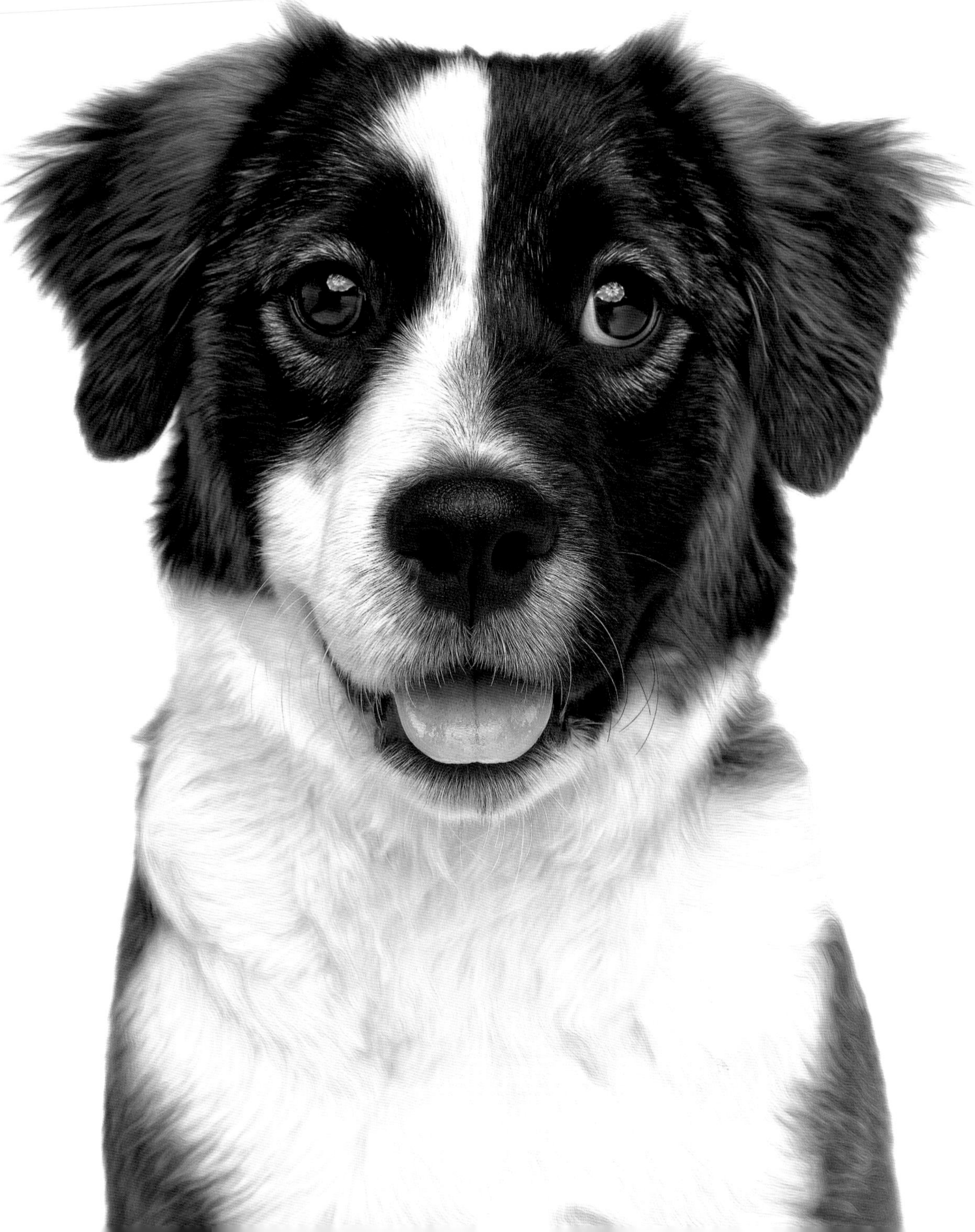

Tex & Maisie

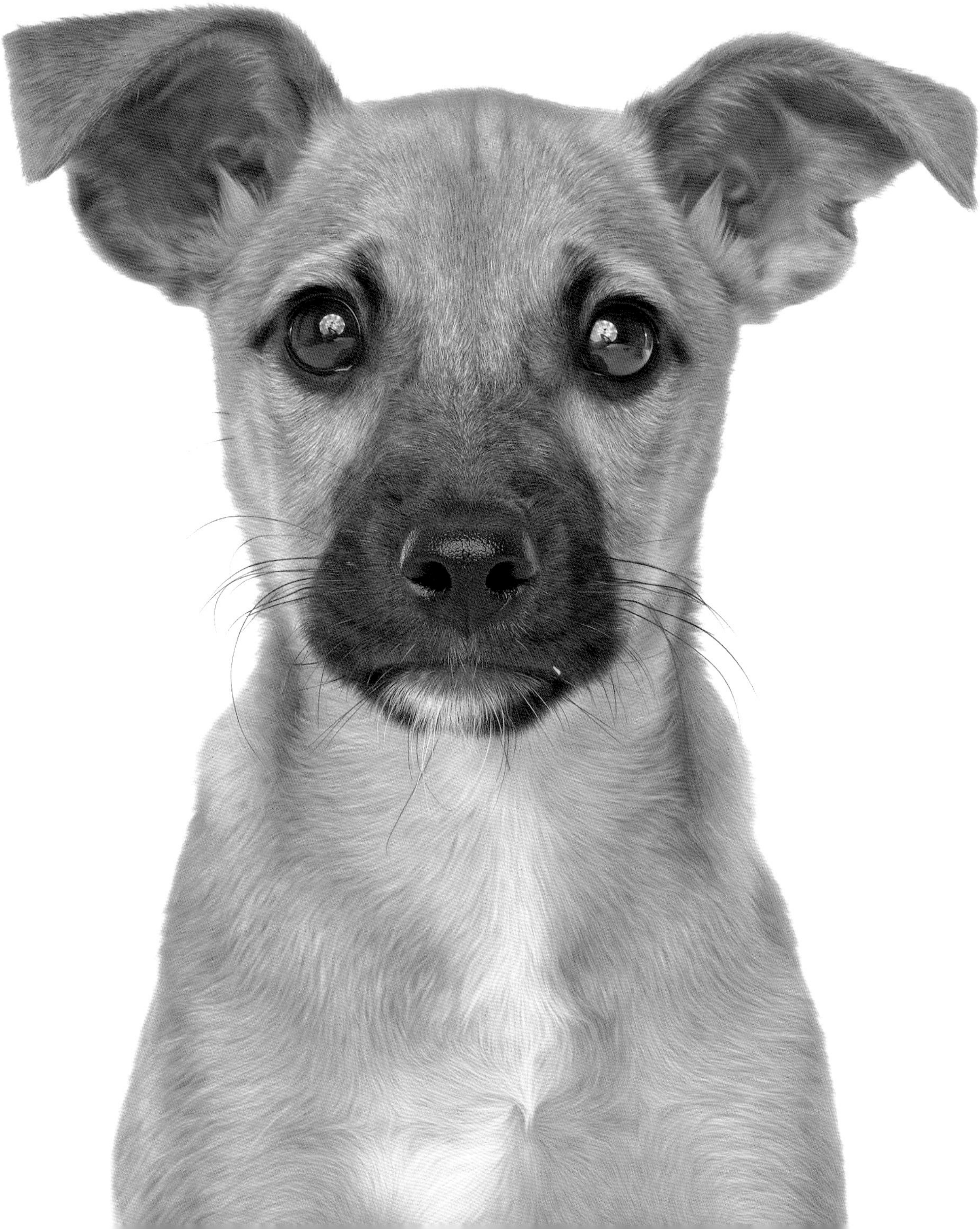

Cody & Oliver

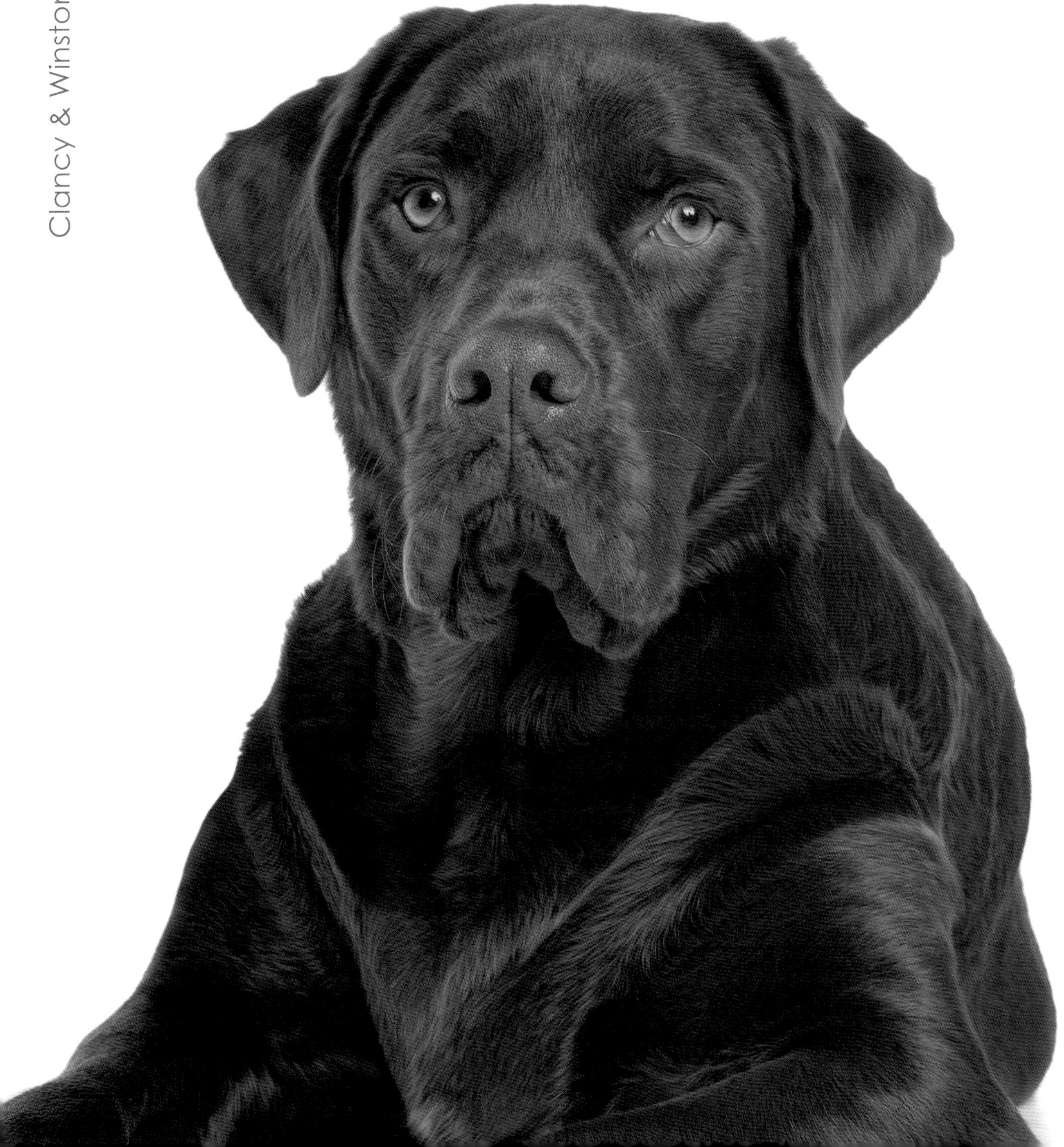

Clancy & Winston

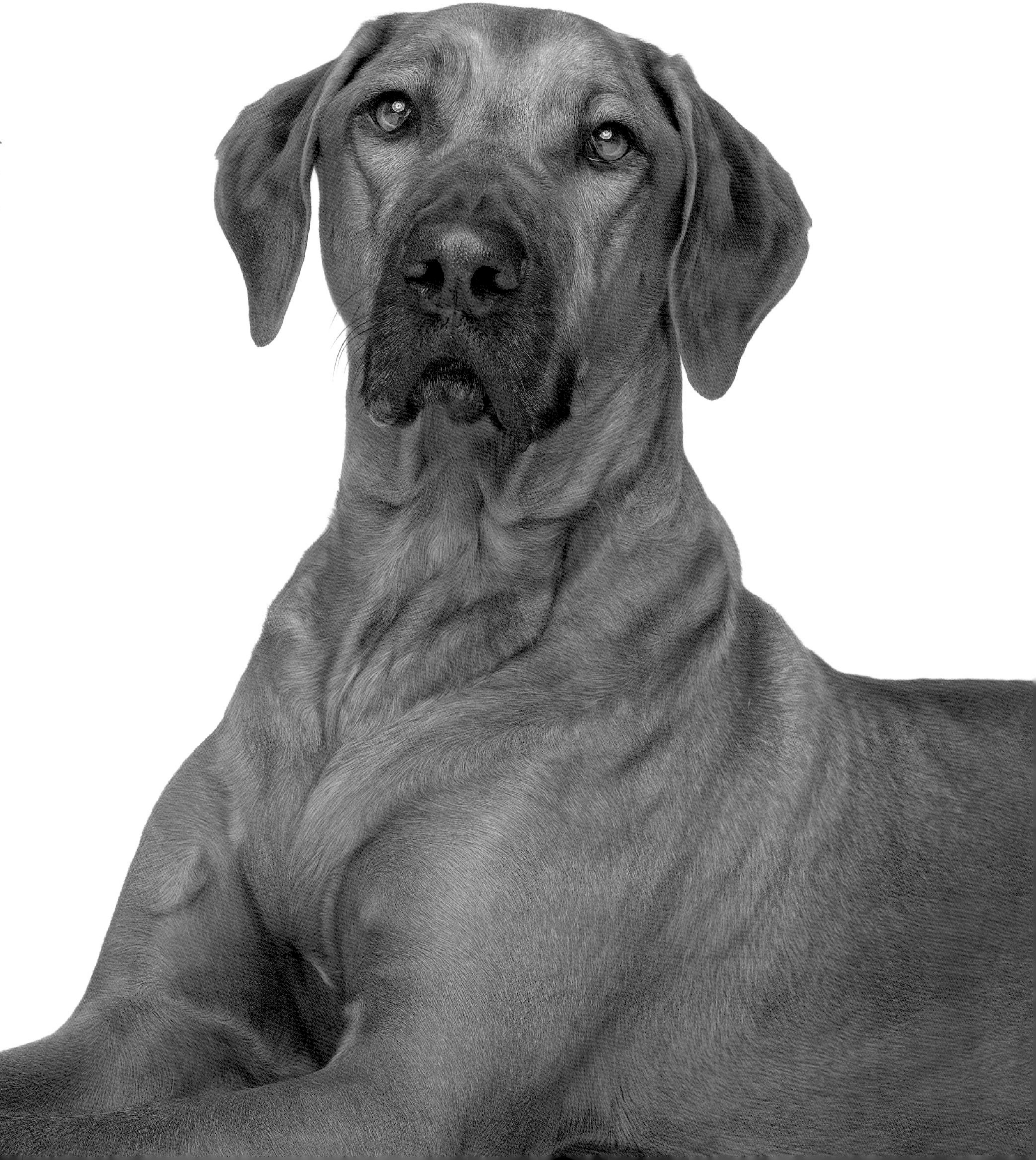

Casey & Safari

Frankenstein & Bruno

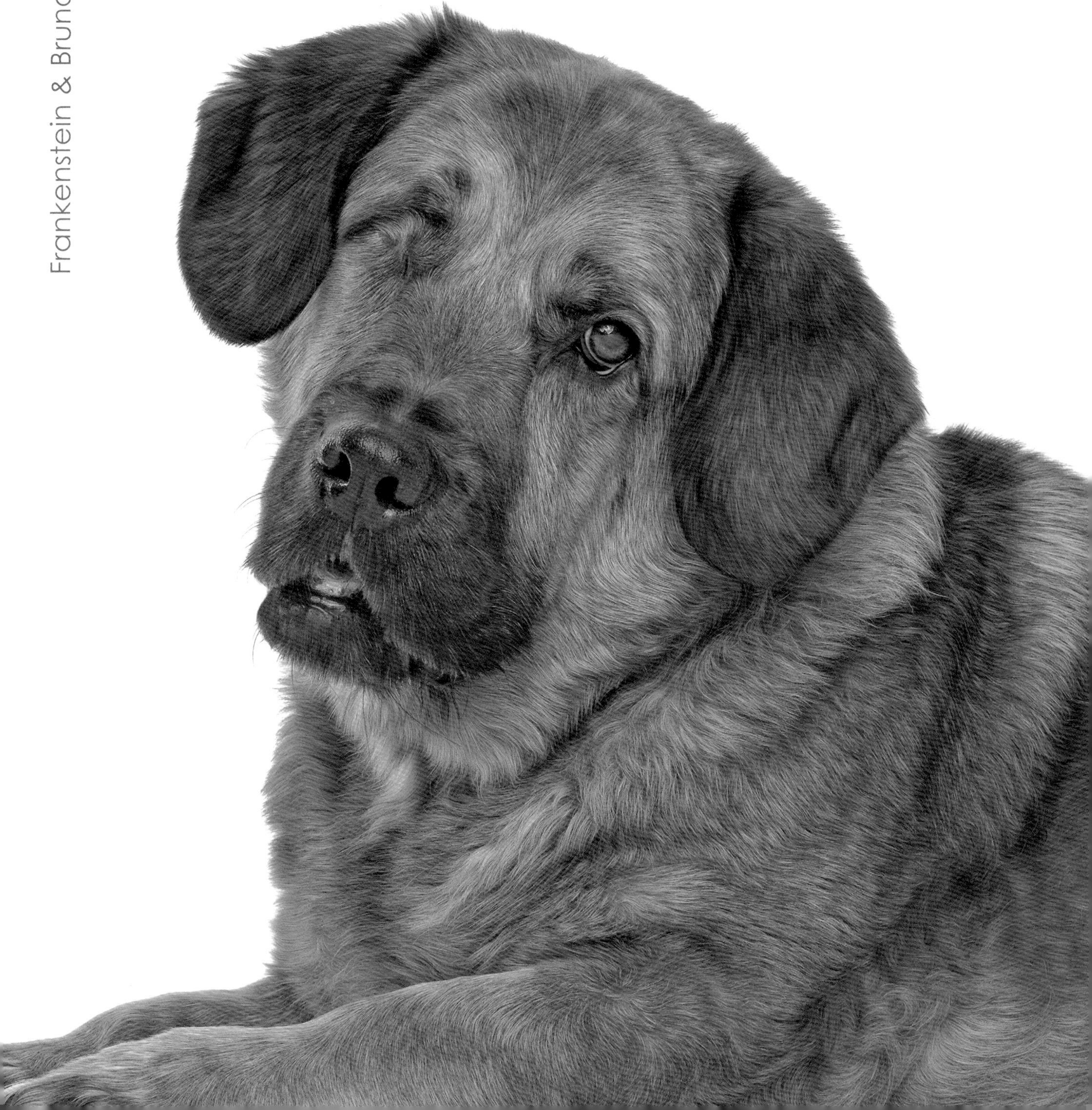

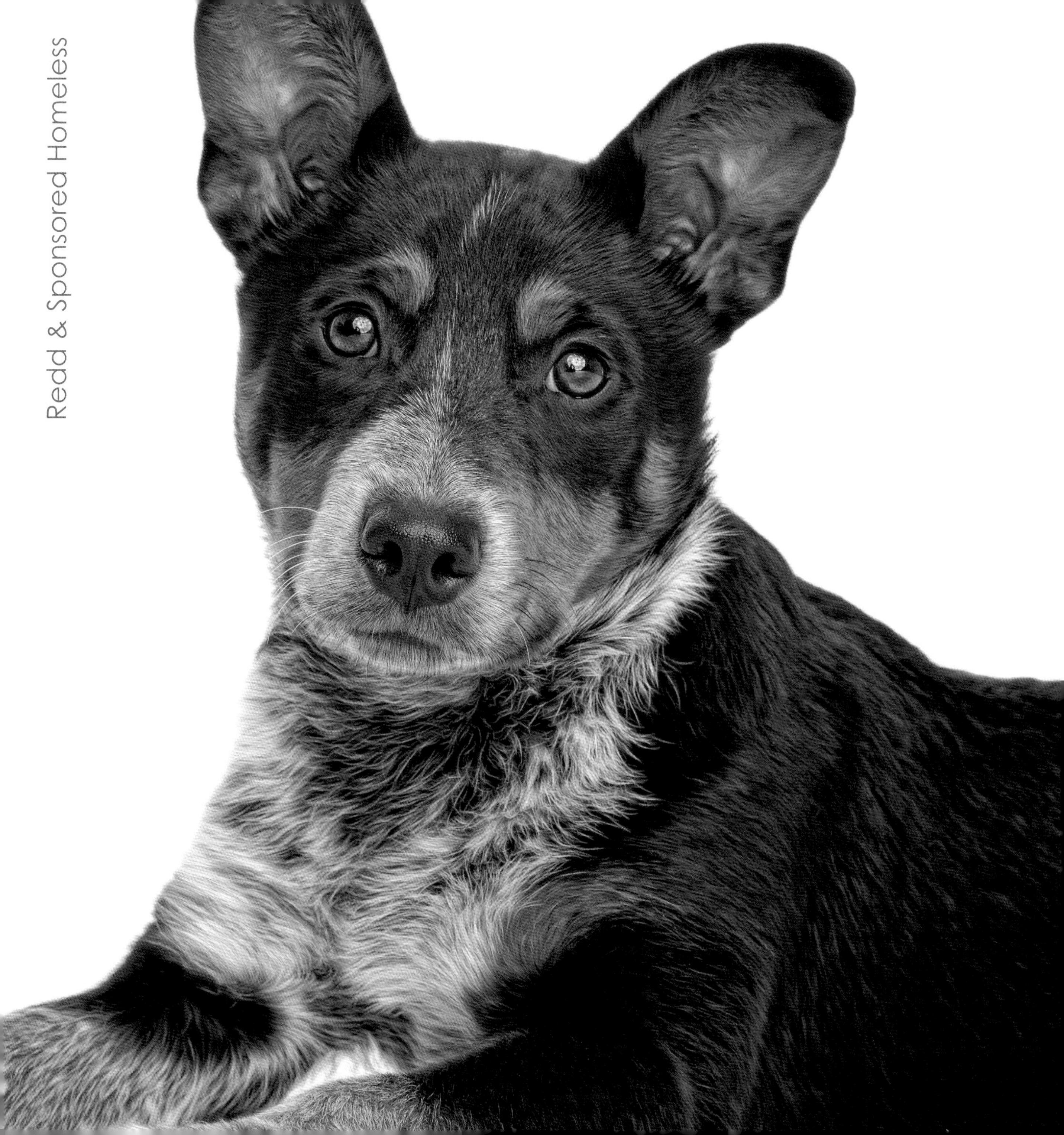

Redd & Sponsored Homeless

Betty & Dixie

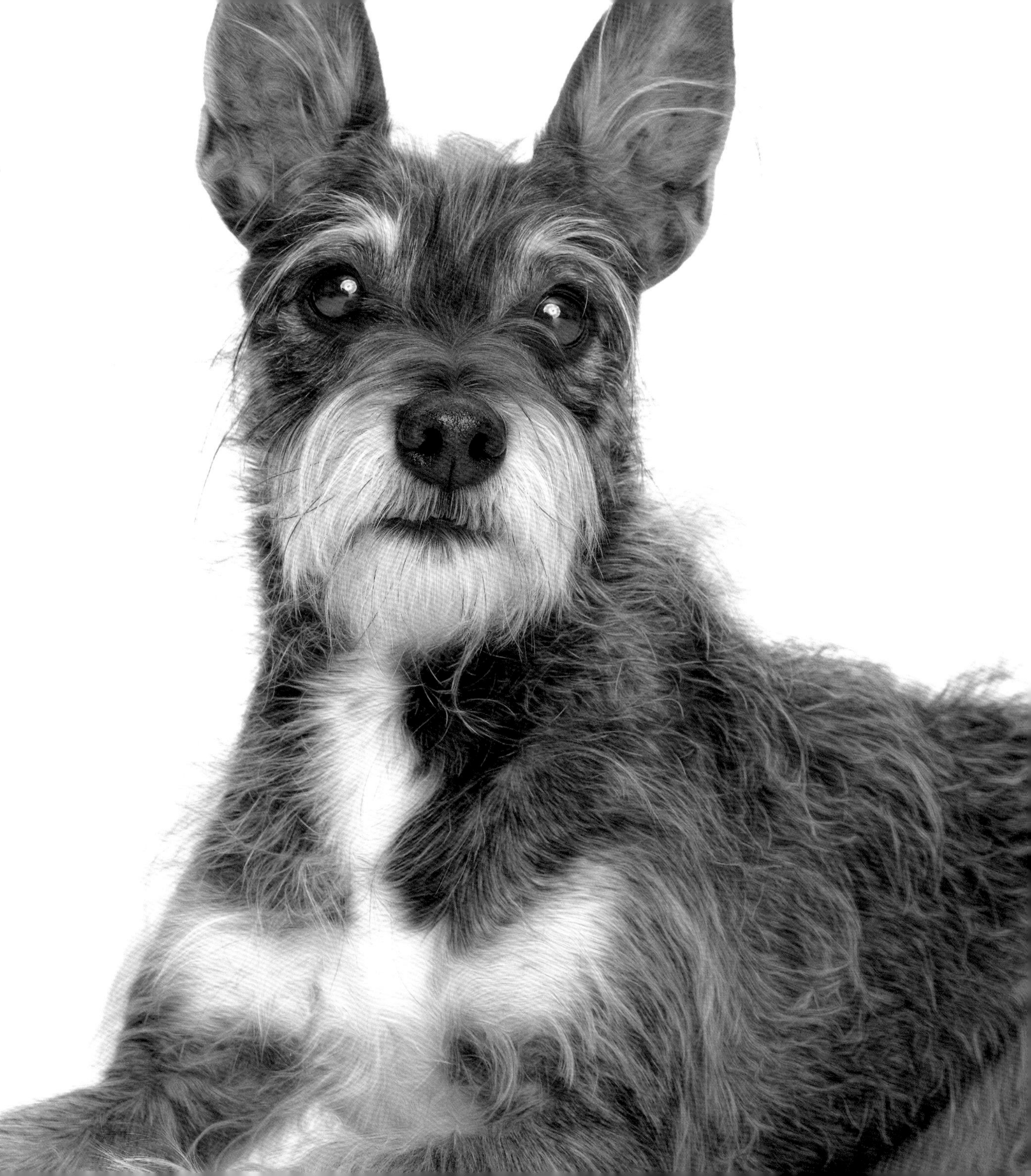

Daisy & Biscuit

Isabella & Bean

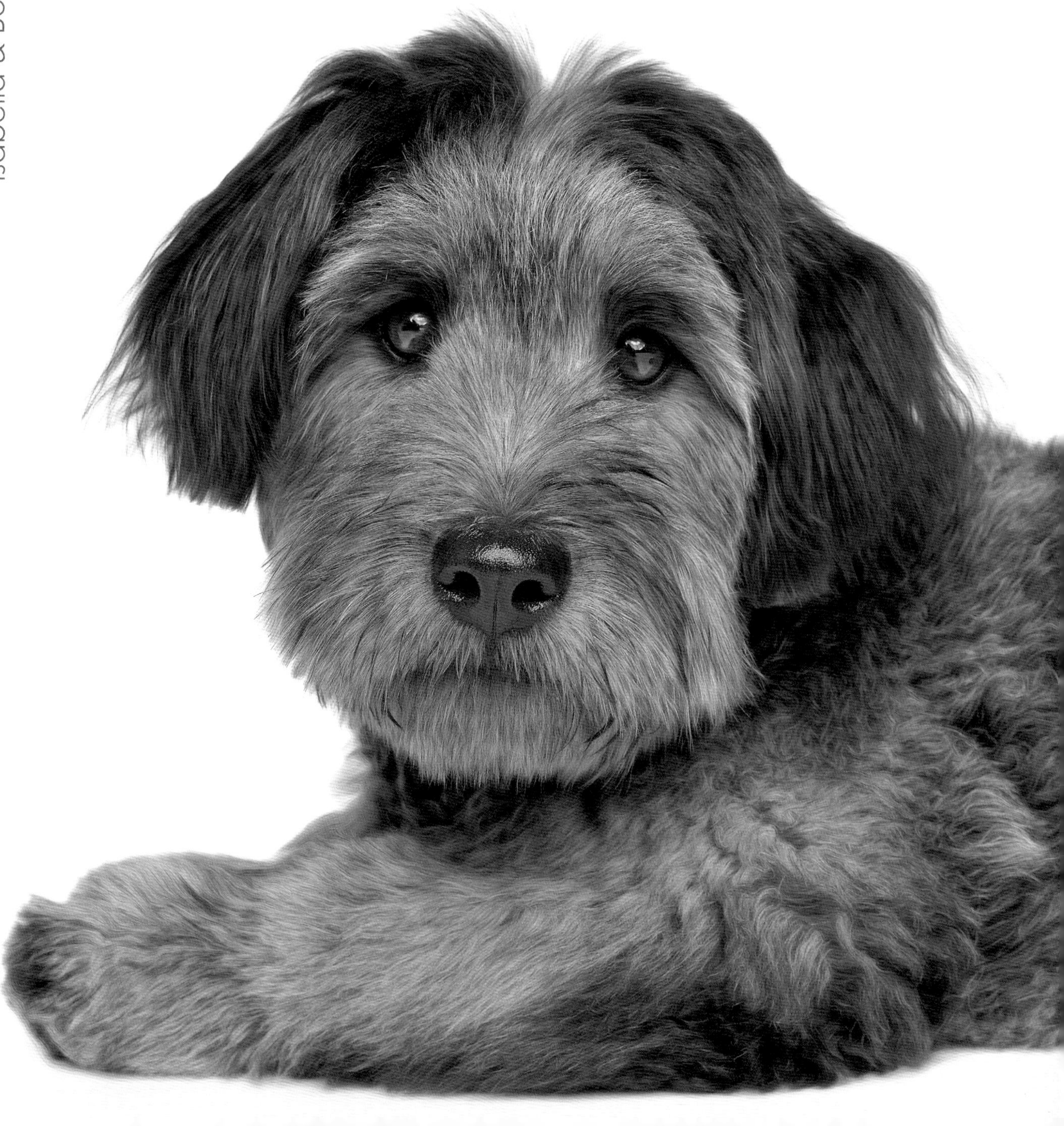

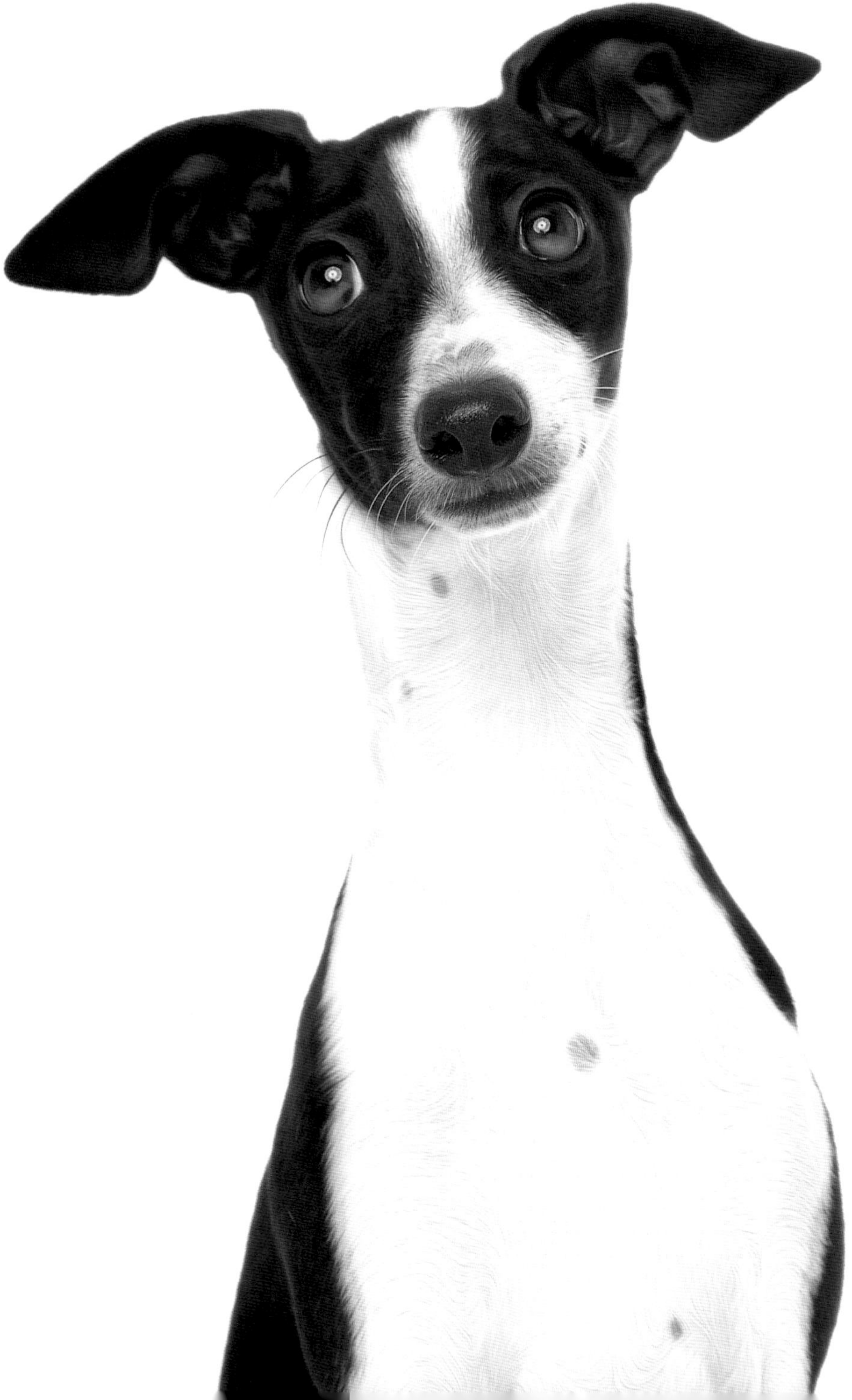

Boo & Wimbledon

Leo & Mini

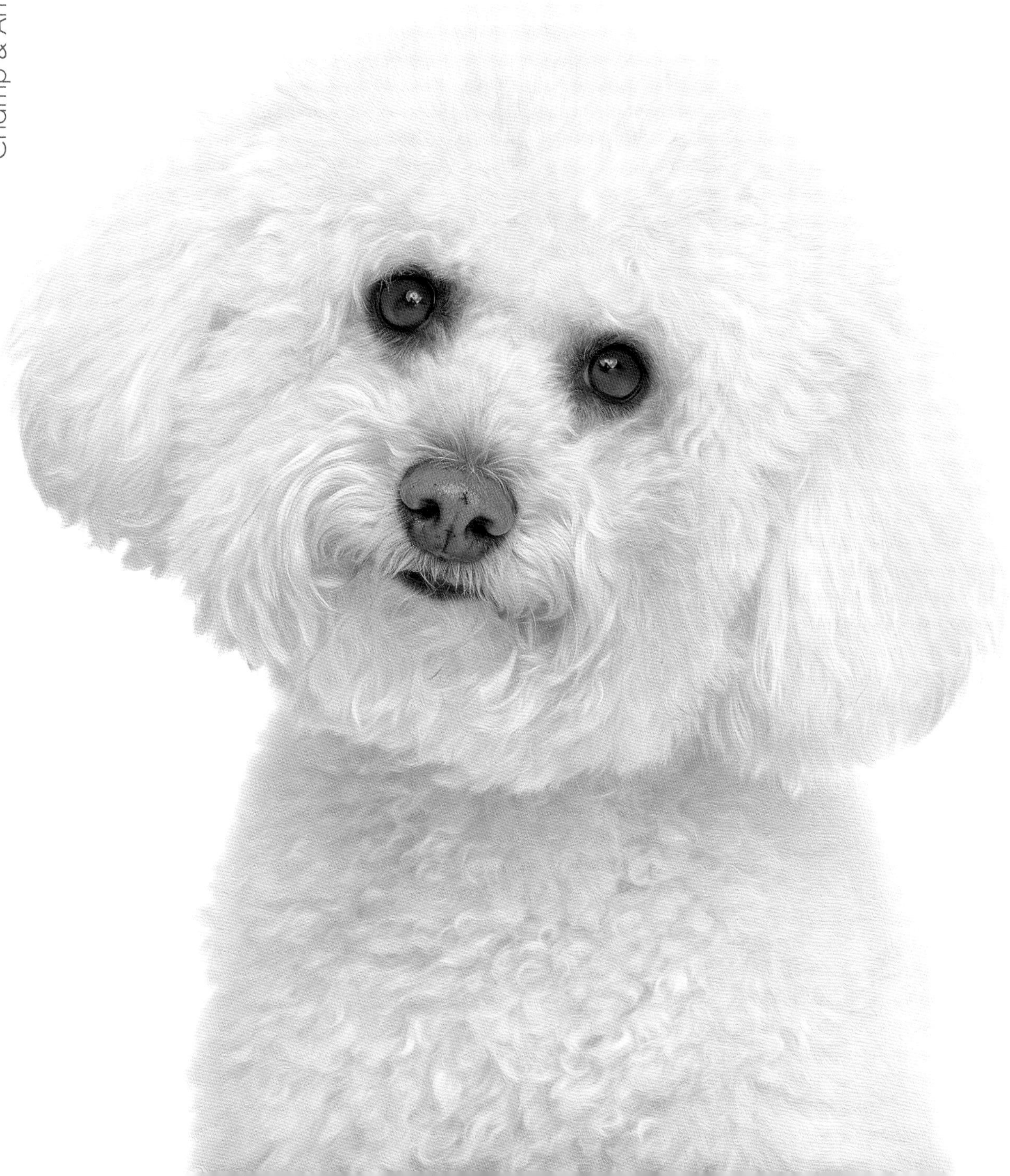

Champ & Arthur

Over $2.5 million donated to pet rescues
Some of the pages in *Rover* are reserved for pet-lovers who make a donation to one of the many deserving rescues we support to have their beloved pet photographed and included on a page in a *Rover* book. This program has generated donations of over $2.5 million for rescues. More importantly, we have bridged countless relationships between effective rescues and generous donors that continue long after *Rover*.

Why some dogs in Rover don't have a name
"Sponsored Homeless" dogs in *Rover* were photographed while living at a rescue to highlight that healthy, smart, beautiful, loving and unique mixed breeds and purebreds are available for adoption at shelters everywhere. Special thanks to all the wonderful donors who sponsored these homeless dogs to help increase their chances of adoption through compelling photography and to help overcome the stigma that shelter dogs are inferior to pets acquired elsewhere. Because of the tireless and effective efforts of the rescues we support, all of the homeless pets in *Rover*, have all been adopted.

Honor your pet. Save a life. Be a hero.
Visit RoverWorks.org to discover how you can make a donation to have your dog, and a homeless dog, photographed and included in a future edition of Rover. It's a wonderful way to honor your best friend while helping homeless pets.

Providing rescues with a way to attract new donors
Selected rescues are able to use their exclusive partnership with *Rover* as a vehicle to bring awareness to their organization and attract new donors.

1/25 Amanda Hedlund

Distinctive limited edition, signed framed art for home, office, hotels & restaurants by Amanda Hedlund & Andrew Grant | RoverWorks.org

rover
RoverWorks.org